TH!NK FOR YOURSELF

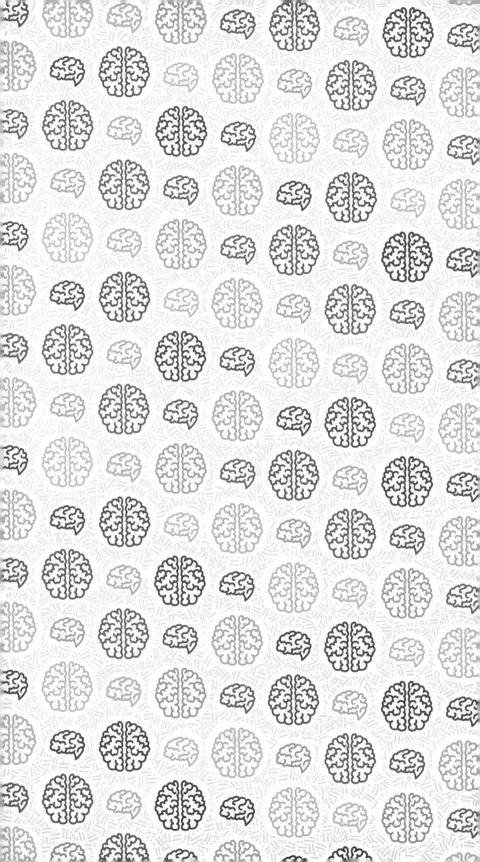

TH!NK FOR YOURSELF

THE ULTIMATE GUIDE TO CRITICAL THINKING IN AN AGE OF INFORMATION OVERLOAD

By Andrea Debbink • Art by Aaron Meshon

duopress

Editor: Heidi Fiedler

Art Director: Violet Lemay

Designer: Thomas Boucher

Library of Congress Cataloging-in-Publication Data available upon request.

ISBN: 9781950500048

duopress books are available at special discounts when purchased in bulk for sales promotions as well as for fund-raising or educational use. Special editions can be created to specification. Contact us at hello@duopressbooks.com for more information.

Manufactured in China

10 9 8 7 6 5 4 3 2 1

Duo Press, LLC

8 Market Place, Suite 300

Baltimore, MD 21202

Distributed by Workman Publishing Company, Inc.

Published simultaneously in Canada by Thomas Allen & Son Limited.

To order: hello@duopressbooks.com

www.duopressbooks.com

www.workman.com

Contents

Introduction

Have you heard of the Stone Age? The Gilded Age? Or the Jazz Age? They're the names of important periods in history. One of the names for the time we're living in right this minute is the Information Age. It means information is available wherever we go and whatever we do. You've probably noticed.

Information is all around. Every day we hear and see messages about what's going on in the world, what to buy, how to dress, what to think, how to feel. These messages come from friends, family, teachers, social media, movies, and music. In short, information is everywhere.

It's easy to experience information overload. Sometimes our minds take in so much information that it's difficult to sort through it. So it just piles up instead, and your mind can start to feel like a messy closet.

WHAT'S ON YOUR MIND?

There's a lot to think about! What's capturing your attention these days?

Music

News

Games

Books

Friends

Crushes

Teachers

Family

Social media

Videos

Texts & messages

Sports

My looks

Technology

My health

What do you do with all this information? How do you sort through and make decisions about it?

It's time to *think* for *yourself!*

"**THINK** for **YOURSELF** and let **OTHERS** ENJOY THE **PRIVILEGE** of **DOING SO** too."

—**VOLTAIRE,** A FRENCH PHILOSOPHER AND WRITER WHO ARGUED FOR EQUAL RIGHTS IN THE 18TH CENTURY

WHAT IS Critical Thinking?

People think all the time. We make plans, worry, relive memories, make decisions, daydream, and more. That's not the kind of thinking this book is about.

This book isn't about *what* to think. (That's up to you!) It's about *how* to think for yourself.

THE BIG IDEA

CRITICAL THINKING IS THE PROCESS OF CAREFULLY EVALUATING IDEAS AND FACTS TO MAKE DECISIONS ABOUT WHAT TO BELIEVE AND DO.

Thinking is a skill—like learning to skateboard or do algebra. The more we practice it, the better we get.

> Wait. I thought being "critical" is a bad thing.

Not always. The word *critical* has a few different definitions. In this case, *critical* means to use careful evaluation or judgment. We can all think critically, and in the Information Age, thinking for yourself is more important than ever.

TIME TO THINK

Some people can live their whole lives without ever learning this important skill. The good news? It's never too late to think critically. And you get a gold star for starting now!

Critical Thinking in Action

It's easier to understand the process with an example. In 1973, the United States government passed a law called the Endangered Species Act. Since then, more than 1,600 animal species have been protected by the law, including the bald eagle, grizzly bear, humpback whale, and many plants and insects.

Deciding which animals should be added to or removed from the list is rarely easy. Often, people disagree about the issue. Ultimately, Congress makes the decision after getting input from experts. Congress recently considered whether the gray wolf should remain on the endangered list.

A hundred years ago, gray wolves were hunted so intensely that there were hardly any left in the United States. After the Endangered Species Act was passed, the gray wolf was added to the list of protected animals. (This meant it became illegal to hunt wolves because there were so few left.) Since that time, wolf populations have recovered, and there are now more than 6,000 wolves in the lower 48 states.

Now that the wolf population has grown, some people would like to remove the gray wolf from the endangered species list. Others think the wolf should stay on the list. Imagine you are a member of Congress and must decide how to vote. Start by going through the process.

ASK QUESTIONS

- Who wants to remove the gray wolf from the endangered species list? Who wants to keep it on the list?
- How many wolves live in the United States? Is this a big or small number?
- What happens when an animal species is removed from the endangered species list?

GATHER EVIDENCE

- Interview people who live near wolves, including farmers, ranchers, and forest rangers.
- Interview people who study wolves.
- Research the topic using the library, books, or the internet.

EVALUATE EVIDENCE

- Check the facts.
- Analyze the data.
- Look out for logical fallacies or errors in logic.

TEST ASSUMPTIONS AND BE OPEN-MINDED

- Are wolves always dangerous?
- How often do wolves kill livestock?
- Will removing the wolves from the list really be bad for wolf populations?

REACH A CONCLUSION

- Decide whether wolves should stay on the list or be removed.

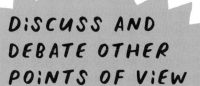

DISCUSS AND DEBATE OTHER POINTS OF VIEW

Chances are, you're not a member of Congress (yet!), and you probably don't have to make a decision like this anytime soon. But, whether you realize it or not, you still use critical thinking every day. Thinking critically isn't always easy. Sometimes it's easier to take shortcuts instead of going through the whole process.

Let's say you walk into your classroom one day and discover you have a substitute teacher. Like many people, you might take one of these unfortunate shortcuts in your mind.

STEREOTYPES

"Uh oh. Ms. Sharpe looks pretty old. I bet she's mean."
A stereotype is a mistaken belief about a whole group of people that's based on how they look or your limited experience with them. The belief that older people are mean or grumpy is a stereotype.

FEAR

"Oh no! Our last sub embarrassed me in front of the whole class!"
Sometimes our fear is based on past experiences. But

whether our fears are based on real dangers or not, fear can get in the way of thinking clearly.

BLIND FAITH

"My sister told me all about Ms. Sharpe. She doesn't care if you leave class without asking."

Someone acting on blind faith assumes he knows all the facts or has all the information he needs. He doesn't take time to think about the possibilities or what the consequences of his beliefs might be.

IGNORANCE

"If she's a sub, she can't know anything about math."

Ignorance, or a lack of knowledge or information, makes it difficult to make good decisions or come to thoughtful conclusions.

JUMPING TO CONCLUSIONS

"A sub? Mr. Chang must be in the hospital!"

Drawing a conclusion without all the facts can lead to wrong conclusions or poor decisions.

Thinking for yourself isn't always a fast process. Sometimes it can take years to reach a conclusion about a certain belief or action. And even then, with new information or experiences, those beliefs can change. Check out some of the beliefs from the past that changed after critical thinking was used.

MAGIC MUD ///////////

Hundreds of years ago, people believed frogs were magically formed out of mud! They called it "spontaneous generation." People believed this because every spring frogs would seem to suddenly appear in ponds and puddles. (You might say they were *jumping* to a conclusion.) But when people started to study frogs more closely, they realized frogs actually came from eggs that turned into tadpoles and then into adult frogs. No magic there.

MIRACLE WATER ///////////

Today we think of sparkling water as a refreshing drink, but at the turn of the 20th century, people thought it was medicine! Back then, doctors didn't know very much about what caused or cured illnesses. Some people noticed that when they drank water that came from a spring (and sometimes that water was naturally bubbly), they seemed to feel better. Others took advantage of this and started selling the water as a miracle cure. We know now that there was nothing miraculous about the water. At the time, many people didn't have reliable indoor plumbing or safe water, so when they drank some of this "miracle" water, not surprisingly, they felt a lot better!

DIY GOLD ///////////

Wouldn't it be great if you could take something ordinary and turn it into gold? That's what alchemists thought too. Beginning in ancient times, alchemists thought it was possible to turn a common metal, such as iron, tin, or copper, into a precious metal, such as gold or silver. It took hundreds of years—and a lot of chemistry—to discover that, sadly, it wasn't actually possible.

CLEVER CHIMPS ///////////

For many years people thought humans were the only animals who used tools. And some people believed that proved humans were better than animals. But in the 1960s, Dr. Jane Goodall studied chimpanzees in the wild. She was the first person to see chimps use tools. Since then, scientists have learned other animals use tools too. (Find out about more Dr. Goodall on page 56.)

QUIZ: WHAT KIND OF THINKER ARE YOU?

You already use your mind every day. Take this quiz to learn more about your thinking style. Then check your answers on page 21.

1. Good news! Your parents just agreed your family can adopt a pet, but they don't know which animal to get. The first thing you do is:
   a. Ask your friends for their opinions.
   b. Do an internet search for all the adoptable pets in your town.
   c. Let your sister pick. She has good ideas.

2. You're working on a group project for school. Two of your group mates get into a disagreement about how to present the project. You:
   a. Ask your teacher for her opinion.
   b. Remember that one of your group mates did an awesome presentation last semester and decide it'd be best to go with her idea.
   c. Listen to both classmates before giving your opinion.

3. You see a news clip of a march happening in Washington, DC. Your first thought is:
   a. "Why is this on the news?"
   b. "I heard my parents talking about this."
   c. "I wonder why these people are marching?"

4. A classmate invites you to his birthday party next weekend, but you're not sure if you should bring a gift. You:
   a. Ask him.
   b. Talk to other people who are going to the party to see if they're bringing gifts.
   c. Decide to bring a gift anyway. You might be the only one but your classmate will like it no matter what.

5. Your favorite T-shirt is missing. Your younger sister has always liked it, but you don't remember her asking to borrow it. You head straight to:
   a. Your desk chair. Maybe you can sit and think about the last place you saw it.
   b. The laundry room. Maybe it's being washed.
   c. Your sister's room. Maybe she borrowed it or knows where it is.

6. Your friends have a great idea for a Halloween group costume! The thing is, you think it might offend some people. You decide to:
   a. Talk to people you think it might offend.

b. Find examples of people wearing this costume in the past and read what was said about it.

c. Decide it's not worth the risk and choose a new costume.

7. On the first day of class, your teacher makes a rule that seems pretty unfair. You:

a. Raise your hand and ask why he made the rule.

b. Ask friends with different teachers if they have the same rule.

c. Decide he must have a good reason for the rule.

8. A good friend is in a bad mood one day, and it seems like you can't do anything right. You:

a. Ask him if he's ok.

b. Think about what's been happening in your friend's life that might make him feel frustrated.

c. Assume he's just having an off day and will be better tomorrow.

9. You've been practicing hard all season, but at Saturday's soccer game, your coach barely lets you play. As you sit on the bench, you:

a. Wonder what you can do to get better.

b. Realize you're not the only one who isn't playing much.

c. Remember that your coach tries to be fair.

ANSWERS

Mostly As: You're a Questioner!

When faced with a tricky decision or situation, your first step is to ask questions. This is such an important skill! But remember not to stop there. Make sure you take the time to find the *answers* to your questions and explore other viewpoints too.

Mostly Bs: You're an Investigator!

When it comes to smart thinking, you dive right into research mode. Part of being a critical thinker is knowing how to find the information you need. But before you dive too deep, take time to make sure you're investigating the right questions. And no matter what evidence you find, keep an open mind!

Mostly Cs: You're a Philosopher!

Your first instinct is to consult other people's points of view and be open-minded. (You're probably a fantastic listener too!) But remember to take the other steps in the thinking process, especially asking good questions and evaluating evidence.

THE BiG iDEA

NONE OF THESE TYPES OF THINKING ARE BETTER THAN THE OTHERS. THE IMPORTANT TAKEAWAY IS THAT A CRITICAL THINKER KNOWS HOW TO DO ALL THREE!

"I LOVE technology, USING my HANDS and BEING PRACTICAL. It's what I LOVE DOING and it KEEPS ME GOING."

—RICHARD TURERE, A YOUNG MAASAI INVENTOR WHO FOUND A CLEVER WAY TO MAKE PEACE WITH THE LIONS IN HIS COMMUNITY

PORTRAIT OF A CRITICAL THINKER

▶ RICHARD TURERE ◀

Richard Turere grew up in a Maasai community in Kenya near a national park full of wildlife. Like many of their neighbors, Richard's family depended on livestock to earn their living. But nearly every night, lions prowled the community, killing the cows and bulls. The lions were simply hunting for food, but for Richard's family and their neighbors, losing livestock meant losing money. Some people in the community thought the only solution was to hunt the lions and kill them. When he was 11 years old, Richard hated lions, but he wanted to find a way to protect his family's livestock without harming these predators. One night, Richard realized that when he carried a flashlight near the livestock pens, the lions would stay away. Richard already knew about electronics. (He even took apart his mom's new radio so he could figure out how it worked!) Richard used his knowledge to come up with an invention he called Lion Lights. Richard installed the flashing solar-powered lights near the livestock pen. And there were no more lion attacks at his family's home! Soon, Richard's neighbors wanted Lion Lights too, and he went to work installing them all around his community. Ten years later, Richard's invention is being used at more than 700 homesteads in Kenya, protecting people, cattle, *and* lions. And what does Richard think about lions today? "I love lions. I don't see why I *shouldn't* love lions."

YOUR TURN

As you read earlier in this chapter, ideas, opinions, and beliefs can change over time. Sometimes the ideas or beliefs that change are big and affect a lot of people. Sometimes the changing ideas or beliefs are small—so small they might affect only one person. Maybe you've seen this happen in your own life. Have you changed your mind in any of these ways?

"**FOCUS MORE** on **LEARNING** than on **SUCCEEDING. INSTEAD** of **PRETENDING** that you **UNDERSTAND SOMETHING** when you **DON'T,** just **RAISE YOUR HAND** and ask a **QUESTION.**"

—**MICHELLE OBAMA,** *THE FIRST AFRICAN AMERICAN FIRST LADY*

Chapter

-2-

Asking Questions

The first step in the critical thinking process is one that comes naturally to humans: asking questions! But some questions lead to more interesting answers than others.

A Diverse World

Diversity is a common word today. You've probably heard it at home, at school, or on social media. *Diversity* means "variety." When it comes to people, caring about diversity means you recognize and respect everyone's unique identities and experiences. When diversity is not valued or when people are not allowed to share their own point of view, stereotypes often show up instead. (We talked a bit about stereotypes on page 14.) A stereotype is a belief about a whole group of people that's based on how they look or on your limited experience with them. Stereotypes are all around. Here are some examples of stereotypes about people. Have you heard any of these?

"All girls like pink."

"All boys are good at sports."

"Girls shouldn't have short hair," or "Boys shouldn't have long hair."

"People from a certain country are lazy."

"People who practice a certain religion are dangerous."

"If a person uses a wheelchair, they probably want a lot of extra help."

TIME TO **THINK**

Have you ever thought about where stereotypes come from? Have you ever done anything that's challenged one of these beliefs? Write about it in a notebook or on a piece of paper. (Don't worry about making a mistake or having the "right" answer. Sometimes writing things down—or even doodling!—can help us think.)

Stereotypes are harmful. One way to challenge stereotypes is to question them. (Asking questions is what this chapter is all about.) Another way to challenge stereotypes is to care about representation. That means making sure that all perspectives get shared and people get to tell their own stories, especially people who haven't had those same opportunities in the past.

It's normal to wonder about the world around us. Some questions are big, and some are small. Sometimes questions can spark debate and argument. Do any of these questions sound familiar to you?

"What's ASMR?"

"Why do some girls wear hijabs?"

"What do the letters in LGBTQ+ stand for?"

"What's a refugee?"

"What happened to the dinosaurs?"

"Why are some people homeless?

"Why can I see the moon during the day?

"When is the best time of day to write?"

"Why do cats sleep so much?"

"Why don't things taste the way they smell?"

"Why do we have Daylight Savings Time?"

What about you? What are some questions you have? Use a notebook or piece of paper to write them down. You might find some questions keep coming up again and again. Let them guide you!

If you want to be a critical thinker, it helps to be curious. Curiosity is the desire to learn and investigate. Explorers, detectives, scientists, artists, journalists, and teachers are all people who use curiosity in their work. They learn by asking questions. Who are some curious people you know?

Questions have *more* to teach us than answers

Sometimes it can be hard to ask questions. When you ask a question, it means admitting you don't have all the information and you don't know everything. Plus, we like answers. Today it's easy to get them in a flash. And it feels good to know the answer. But sometimes, asking the right question can unlock the answer you've been looking for.

Critical thinkers ask lots of questions. We can't know exactly what sparked some of the world's greatest discoveries and innovations, but we can imagine deep thinkers may have asked questions like these:

"What's it like to travel on a beam of light?"
—Albert Einstein

"What happens if you combine Western and Indian music?"
—Philip Glass

"Why must women follow the laws when they have no voice in making them?"
—Elizabeth Cady Stanton

"How can we make zoo habitats better for lizards and reptiles?"
—Joan Beauchamp Procter

Or consider this simple question that a mother asked her daughter over a plate of pancakes on an ordinary day:

If you could change one thing in the new year, what would it be?

I'd make it so that kids in my class, in my grade —that kids everywhere— could read books with black girls as the main characters.

This question—and her answer—led the girl, Marley Dias, to launch a campaign to draw attention to the lack of diversity in children's books. To date, Marley's #1000blackgirlbooks campaign has collected more than 9,000 books that feature girls of color as the main characters.

QUIZ: QUESTION YOUR QUESTION

When you need to make up your mind about something (or take action), first figure out what question you're trying to answer. Then read this checklist. For each "yes" answer, give yourself one point. (Use your fingers to keep track.)

☐ Are you uncertain of the answer to your question?
☐ Does your question have a purpose?
☐ Does your question require more than a "yes" or "no" answer?
☐ Is your question deep?
☐ Is your question specific?
☐ Will your question encourage conversation?
☐ Is your question short?
☐ Is your question easy to understand?
☐ Is your question free from opinion or bias?
☐ Does your question lead to more questions?
☐ Is your question about a rhinoceros? (Just kidding! No points for this one. Sorry!)

HOW MANY POINTS DO YOU HAVE?

If you got 0–4 points, you're asking a Curious Question. Finding the answer is likely to be easy—and maybe entertaining.

If you got 4–7 points, you're asking an Interesting Question. This kind of question may lead to more questions.

If you got 8–10 points, you're asking a Wise Question. You may be asking a question that people have been thinking about for thousands of years. You might not find an answer, but you're sure to learn something!

THE BIG IDEA

ASKING THE RIGHT QUESTION CAN REVEAL THE HEART OF THE ISSUE. SPENDING MORE TIME IN THIS STAGE OF THE CRITICAL THINKING PROCESS CAN MAKE THE OTHER STEPS MORE SUCCESSFUL.

"**AS A GIRL** with a **DISABILITY,** I **KNOW** that **MY STORY** is not **a SAD ONE.**"

—**MELISSA SHANG,** *A YOUNG WRITER WHO ADVOCATES FOR PEOPLE WITH DISABILITIES*

PORTRAIT OF A CRITICAL THINKER

MELISSA SHANG

For Melissa Shang, it all started with a question: *Why are people with disabilities shown only in one way?* When Melissa was 10 years old, she realized certain characters were missing among the toys she owned and the stories she read: kids like her. She owned a lot of dolls, but none had a wheelchair. She read a lot of books, but the characters with disabilities were never the main characters and their lives were often sad. Melissa had muscular dystrophy, used a wheelchair—and had a *happy* life. A life with friends, hobbies, and homework. Where was that girl in the books she read? Melissa made a plan. She wrote to her favorite toy company asking them to consider creating a doll with a story like hers, and then she started a petition. Her petition made headlines, but the toy company didn't honor Melissa's request. For Melissa, that wasn't the end. She decided to create the character and write a book herself. But publishers turned her down too. Melissa still didn't give up. She created a Kickstarter campaign and self-published a book with her sister. It's a story about Mia, the girl that Melissa always wanted to read about. Since then, Melissa has written an essay for the *New York Times*,

YOUR TURN

Ask your family and friends to answer some of the questions below. Some are serious, some are silly, but either way they'll make you think and give you something to talk about! These are perfect for mealtimes, long car trips, and even your journal or notebook—whenever you want to have some time to think.

If you could change one thing about your school, what would it be and why?

What makes you feel brave?

given a TED talk, introduced Pakistani activist Malala Yousafzai when she won the Liberty Medal, and continues to be an outspoken advocate for people with disabilities. And it all started with a question.

If hamsters could talk, what would they say and why?

If you could become a character in any book or movie, who would it be and why?

Would you rather be able to jump like a cat or run like a dog? Why?

Would you rather travel back in time or travel to the future? What year?

What makes someone a good friend?

Would you rather sleep on a pile of marshmallows or a pile of gummy bears? Why?

"**LOOK UP** at **THE STARS** and not **DOWN** at **YOUR FEET. TRY** to make **SENSE** of **WHAT** you see and **WONDER** about **WHAT** makes the **UNIVERSE EXIST. BE CURIOUS.**"

—STEPHEN HAWKING, A PHYSICIST

KNOWN FOR HIS WORK ON BLACK HOLES

Chapter
-3-

Gathering Evidence

Once you've figured out what question you're asking, it's time to start gathering evidence, so you can learn more about whatever subject you're interested in. We all have places we turn to first when we look for answers. You probably have favorite books, magazines, websites, podcasts, and even librarians who help you learn about new subjects. Those are good sources to turn to. But when you want to dig deeper, you may need to expand your search for answers. And keep your eyes open for evidence that might contradict your own ideas too!

The Environment

You've probably spent your whole life hearing about melting polar ice, carbon footprints, and warming oceans. The environment is an important topic and one that brings up a lot of emotions and opinions in people. Not everyone agrees that climate change matters. And not everyone agrees on the best ways to respond to it. Do we stop using fossil fuels (like gasoline) and switch to electric cars? Should governments make rules about how we use water? Should everyone stop using plastic bags? Some answers come more easily than others. With issues like the environment, it can be easy to let our emotions (including our fear) get the best of us. It's ok to feel strong emotions about the things that matter to us. But when facing big issues and thorny questions, it's also important to stay the course in our thinking process. When faced with questions that have complicated consequences, it becomes especially important to gather evidence.

TIME TO THINK

Find three news stories about the environment. (Look for national news sources that present both sides of an issue.) Then set them aside while you finish reading this chapter. You'll need them for the activity on page 60.

How to Gather Evidence

Evidence is the information that helps you find an answer or make a decision. There are three steps to follow when gathering evidence.

1. Find information.

2. Make connections.

3. Draw conclusions from the connections.

In other words, gathering evidence is like doing a dot-to-dot puzzle.

Let's say you're an ancient adventurer looking up at a night sky full of stars. (Hundreds of years ago, people often used the stars to guide them at night.)

1. When you first look at the sky, all you see are many bright dots of light.

2. But then you draw lines between the stars, connecting them to each other.

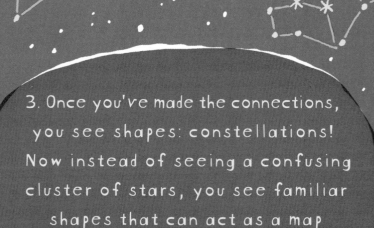

3. Once you've made the connections, you see shapes: constellations! Now instead of seeing a confusing cluster of stars, you see familiar shapes that can act as a map to guide you.

Now that we've got the big picture, let's go back to the first step: finding information. Evidence is made up of facts and observations. There are two types of evidence.

Qualitative evidence refers to how something can be described. Quantitative evidence refers to a number or measurement. It's often called *data*.

QUALITATIVE EVIDENCE

1 The soccer balls are blue and white.

2 The team is outside.

3 The team's name is the Thunderbolts.

THE BIG IDEA

EVIDENCE IS ANYTHING THAT HELPS SOMEONE PROVE OR UNDERSTAND THE TRUTH. DATA IS A TYPE OF EVIDENCE THAT INCLUDES MEASUREMENTS, STATISTICS, AND OTHER NUMBERS THAT CAN BE USED TO CALCULATE AND REASON. EVIDENCE AND DATA—ALONG WITH THOUGHTS AND FEELINGS—ARE USED TO DRAW CONCLUSIONS.

QUANTITATIVE EVIDENCE

4 There are 15 people in this picture.

5 There are 13 kids and 2 adults.

6 5 people are sitting down.

How to Gather Evidence

Let's say you're doing a science project on an environmental topic. Maybe one of your research questions is "How does garden fertilizer affect local animals and insects?" The first step to finding an answer is to gather evidence. No matter what question you're asking or what topic you're exploring, here are some ways to gather evidence.

Make observations.

Interview experts.

Read about the topic.

Do an internet search.

Ask people to take a survey or poll.

Hold a focus group.

Conduct experiments.

Research historical records and documents.

What Are Sources?

A source is anything or anyone that provides information. A primary source is often someone who witnessed something firsthand. (Primary sources aren't always people, though. Items such as a diary or a piece of clothing from an important event can also be primary sources. They are direct evidence of what happened.)

Let's say there's a protest march against climate change. You and your friend are planning to go (yay!). But you get sick the day of the march, and your friend has to go without you (ugh!). After, if you wanted to know what the march was like, where would you find that information? You could read about it online or look at social media (those are secondary sources), but for the most reliable information, you would probably just want to ask your friend who was actually at the march.

Not all sources have equal authority, and not all sources are trustworthy. No matter if a source is a primary or secondary source, it's always a good idea to explore how trustworthy or reliable the source is. That's what the next chapter is all about!

QUIZ: WHAT KIND OF INVESTIGATOR ARE YOU?

What do you do when you have a burning question or puzzling problem? Take this quiz to discover your sleuthing style!

1. In history class, your teacher announces that everyone has to do a project about a big event from the 20th century. Your first stop is:
    a. The school library. The librarian always points you in the right direction.
    b. Your great-aunt's house. She's always telling stories about her childhood.
    c. The internet. You want to find a list of history's greatest events.

2. You and your parents disagree about what kind of dog to get. You want a beagle, but your dad says that beagles *always* run away. You don't quite believe him, so you decide to figure out what's true by:
    a. Checking out a book about beagles.
    b. Asking a classmate who has a beagle.
    c. Looking up statistics about beagle behavior.

3. Some friends are coming over for a movie night! You pick a movie that:

a. Has a cool trailer.

b. Everyone in your class has been talking about.

c. Has the best rating.

4. It took a long time, but you *finally* saved up enough of your allowance to buy those sneakers you've been eyeing. Now what?

a. Head to the store! You've been reading about these shoes for months.

b. Get your friend's opinion about how these sneakers will look on you.

c. Compare prices at different stores and websites to make sure you get the best deal. You want money left over!

5. Your scout troop wants to do a community-service project for Earth Day. Everyone has to bring a list of project ideas to the next meeting. Before you brainstorm, what do you do?

a. Check out a neighborhood website to see what kind of projects other people are doing.

b. Ask your parents if they know about any organizations that need volunteers.

c. Look up the top five projects that scout troops usually do for Earth Day.

6. You want to take your bike for a spin, but the pedal is broken. How do you fix it?

    a. Watch a video about how to fix it.

    b. Ask a parent to help.

    c. Look up the part number and price and start saving for a new one.

7. You want to sign up for the city swim team this summer but the swim meets are right before your Maker Club meetings—on the other side of town. To help make your decision you:

    a. Look up how many swim meets you're allowed to miss.

    b. Talk to your friends about what you should do.

    c. Calculate the drive time from the pool to your Maker Club meeting. You can totally get there in time!

8. You've started taking guitar lessons, so now you can finally learn how to play your favorite song! You decide to:

    a. Find a recording so you can listen and learn.

    b. Ask your guitar teacher to help you figure it out.

    c. Look up the guitar chords online.

IF YOU GOT...

Mostly As: You're a Classic Researcher!

When you need information, your first instinct is to hit the books—or internet or anything else you can read! Just be careful to check your sources and not believe everything you read. (More on that soon!)

Mostly Bs: You're a Social Scientist!

When you're looking for answers, you know right where to turn: to other people! Whether it's your friends, parents, or experts, you depend on getting helpful information from other people.

Mostly Cs: You're a Number Cruncher!

When you're in research mode, you head first to the quantitative data—numbers, statistics, and probabilities. This can give you a great foundation, but remember that numbers don't always tell the whole story.

"WHAT YOU DO makes a **DiFFERENCE,** and you have to **DECiDE** what kind of **DIFFERENCE YOU** want to **MAKE."**

—**DR. JANE GOODALL,** *A SCIENTIST ADMIRED FOR HER FIELDWORK ON CHIMPANZEES AND ENVIRONMENTAL ACTIVISM*

PORTRAIT OF A CRITICAL THINKER

DR. JANE GOODALL

Today Dr. Jane Goodall is one of the most celebrated scientists and conservationists of our time. But in the 1960s, she was just an adventurous young woman with a curious mind. When Dr. Goodall was 26 years old, she traveled to the Gombe Stream Nature Reserve (now Gombe National Park in present-day Tanzania) to study chimpanzees. At the time, people didn't know very much about chimpanzees other than what they saw on TV or in movies. Dr. Goodall's research was very difficult at first, and she didn't have any field experience or a college degree. To make matters worse, the chimpanzees wouldn't come near her or any other human. After many months, the chimps finally started to trust Dr. Goodall. She continued to study chimpanzees for more than 50 years and made many surprising discoveries. The first— and most controversial—was that chimps used tools. Up until that point, people thought that humans were the only animals capable of using tools. (See page 17 to understand why this was such a big deal.) Dr. Goodall also learned that chimps express emotion, live in family groups, and eat both plants and meat. Eventually, she learned that the chimps' habitat was in danger and took steps to protect it. Dr. Goodall's work with chimpanzees gave her the desire to help wildlife around the world and teach others about caring for the planet.

Many of Dr. Goodall's accomplishments came from her ability to be a critical thinker and careful researcher. She arrived in Gombe National Park with many questions about chimpanzees and their behavior, such as: How do chimpanzees behave in the wild? What do they eat? How do chimps communicate with each other? Here are some of the ways she gathered evidence to help her find the answers.

MAKING OBSERVATIONS ///////////

When Dr. Goodall first arrived at Gombe, she sat in the dense jungle with her notebook for up to 12 hours a day (!), writing down anything and everything she saw. The chimps were afraid, but Dr. Goodall was patient and persistent.

MAKING (MORE!) OBSERVATIONS /////////

Dr. Goodall worked with a filmmaker to document the chimps' behavior.

CONDUCTING EXPERIMENTS ////////////

Using bananas—one of the chimps' favorite foods—she conducted experiments that helped her understand chimps' abilities.

INTERVIEWING EXPERTS //////////

Over the years, Dr. Goodall worked alongside (and interviewed) other researchers and people who lived in the area where the chimps also made their home.

STUDYING THE TOPIC //////////

Dr. Goodall went back to school in 1962 to get her PhD in ethology, the study of animal behavior.

YOUR TURN

Remember the news articles you found at the beginning of the chapter? It's time to put them to use. Read each article. Then answer the following questions. (Write down the answers on a separate piece of paper.)

What's the name or headline of the article?

Who wrote the article?

TIME TO **THINK**

Which of Dr. Goodall's methods do you think was the most important? Which sounds the most interesting to you?

Highlight any qualitative evidence.

Highlight any quantitative evidence.

How does the article make you feel? Why?

What does the article make you think about? Why?

Does the article use any primary sources?

Does the article use any secondary sources?

"The **TRUTH** is **MORE** **important** than the **FACTS.**"

—**FRANK LLOYD WRIGHT**, AN ARCHITECT KNOWN FOR HIS CREATIVITY AND CONNECTION TO THE LAND

Chapter —4—

Evaluating Evidence

When it comes to critical thinking, simply gathering information isn't enough. What you do with that information matters. If you're trying to draw a conclusion or make a decision, evidence is what will help you get there. Think of it as the fuel for your thinking journey. But not all evidence has equal value or authority. And not all evidence is helpful or relevant. It's like breakfast. Doctors tell us that the food we eat in the morning matters because it gives us energy for the day ahead. A glazed donut and a bowl of oatmeal are both breakfast foods, but they don't have the same nutritional value or effect on our energy levels. Evidence works the same way. Some information is fuel that will help us reach a decision. Other information distracts or misleads. This chapter explains how we can think about information and decide if it's important or valuable.

Social Media

For many people, social media is part of everyday life. And even when it's not, the things that happen on social media affect our larger communities and culture. Social media has become such a big part of our daily habits that scientists, psychologists, and doctors have started to study it. Each day, more information is available about how social media affects people and communities. A quick internet search reveals the many pros and cons of using this technology.

Yet, despite all this information, people often disagree about the role social media should play in our lives. Some people say it can be addictive and hurt our real-life relationships. Other people say social media helps us connect and communicate with others. We have access to the same information. So why do people still disagree about whether social media is good or bad?

THE BiG iDEA

PEOPLE USE EViDENCE iN DiFFERENT WAYS. CRiTiCAL THiNKERS EVALUATE THE iMPORTANCE, ACCURACY, AND RELEVANCY OF iNFORMATiON.

Let's look at social-media use. Here are some thoughts that different people may have about it.

@Teen

"All my friends use social media. Without it, how would I know what's going on?"

@YouTubeCelebrity

"I got my big break on social media!"

@Parent

"I like using social media to stay connected with my family. But I wish my kids didn't use it so much."

@SciencePro

"Social media isn't necessary for our lives. It's just entertainment. We should limit our use of it."

@Dog

#nocomment

@misinformation

"As long as I get the likes, I can say whatever I want."

One reason people come to different conclusions is they have unique points of view and experiences that influence the way they think about specific issues. (We'll get to this in chapter 5.) Another reason people with the same evidence draw different conclusions is that they evaluate the evidence differently. (Or sometimes people don't evaluate evidence at all. Yikes.)

Imagine you heard on social media that cats can bark like dogs. They just choose not to most of the time. Your first step is to do some basic fact-checking.

Fact-Checking 101

A fact is a statement that can be verified, while an opinion is a statement of belief.

"Apples have more than 4 grams of fiber per serving" is a fact.

(You can verify this.)

(This cannot be verified.)

"Apples are the world's best fruit" is an opinion.

When you fact-check information, it means you research it to figure out if it can be verified. Numbers, dates, names, and other details are relatively easy to check. But you'll also want to think about the conclusions that are drawn and if the main idea makes sense as a whole. Here are some questions to ask when you're fact-checking.

1. What's the source of the information?

In the barking cats example, the source is a tweet.

2. Is the source a primary or secondary source?

The person who sent the tweet hasn't actually heard a cat bark. She read about it somewhere. She's a secondary source.

3. If the source isn't a primary source, can you find a primary source?

Yes, the person who sent the tweet links to the website where she found the article. The article is also a secondary source. But the article includes an interview with a veterinarian who has heard cats bark. The vet is the primary source.

4. Does the primary source match what your secondary source (the tweet) told you?

Yes, the veterinarian confirms what the tweet said.

5. Are the primary and secondary sources trustworthy?

In this case, does the article have an author? Does the website appear to have a reputation for factual information? Is the veterinarian in the article a real person who is really a veterinarian?

6. Can I find other sources that support the primary source's evidence?

Yes, you're able to find other articles that provide similar information about barking cats, including other cat experts. Plus, you're able to find a few videos of cats barking.

How to Spot Fake News

The digital world is full of information. But have you ever thought about how easy it is to spread false information? Videos can be faked with editing apps. Online articles that look like news stories might actually be trying to sell you a product. Or worse! They might be meant to mislead or scare people. Even "news" stories can't always be trusted.

So what do we do?

Here's an example of a fake news
story that was repeatedly
shared on social media during
President Obama's time in
office. The story was completely
made up, but many people believed it was true and
kept sharing it on social media. Fake stories just like
this continue to be shared today.

Not all articles you see online are factual or created by
trustworthy sources. It's important to be able to tell the
difference between advertising (sponsored content), real
news stories, and fake news stories. Anytime you read
an article, ask yourself the following questions. (Practice
with the fake news article on the next page.)

1. Who wrote the article?

Ads or fake news stories often omit the author's name.

President Obama Signs Executive Order Banning Pledge of Allegiance

In a surprising move this week, President Obama signed an executive order banning the Pledge of Allegiance at all sporting events and public schools. Lawmakers on both sides of the aisle were stunned. "We were definitely caught off guard," says a senator who wishes to remain anonymous. "But we plan to take it to court. The freedom to recite the pledge should never be taken away from anyone." Under the new ban, anyone who is caught reciting the pledge in public or encouraging others to do so will be subject to a $10,000 fine or up to 6 months in jail. At a press conference this morning, the President admitted that it was a difficult decision but said that he thought the language used in the pledge was "divisive" and created a "hostile environment" at sporting events. "The president was left with no other option," Vice President Biden told reporters. "This is something that should've happened long ago."

Like   Comment   Share

2. Can you find a bio for the writer?

Even if an author is listed, it's not necessarily the name of a real person. Try to find out more information about the author to see if he or she is real and trustworthy.

3. Has the writer written other articles that you're able to find?

This will help determine if the author is real and can be trusted.

4. What claims does the article make?

See if you can figure out the article's main idea and spot different statements that the author is making. Are these facts that you can check? Do they make sense together?

5. Where was the article published?

Some websites and sources are more trustworthy than others. It's also important to be aware of the bias that a source might have.

6. How does it make you feel?

It's normal to feel emotions like anger, fear, and joy when reading an article or watching a video. Real news stories can tap into our emotions just like advertising and fake news can. The difference with fake news is that its main purpose is to make you feel intense emotions such as anger or fear.

Fact-checking is an important step. But when you're evaluating evidence, you'll also want to dig deeper and look at what's being argued. In logic, an argument isn't a debate or angry conversation. It's a series of statements that are meant to support a particular conclusion.

Fallacies

An important part of evaluating evidence is recognizing the arguments that are being made. *Logical fallacies* are errors in thinking that weaken or discredit an argument. Like stereotypes, they're the lazy (and confused) way out of an argument. There are many types of logical fallacies. Let's use the statement, "I think social media should be outlawed because it's easy to misuse it," and see how someone might respond using the most common fallacies.

AD HOMINEM //////////

Ad hominem is Latin for "to the man." This type of argument focuses on attacking a person rather than addressing that person's own argument or claim.

> Well, you're a technophobe!

STRAW MAN //////////

This type of argument misrepresents or exaggerates the ideas people are debating.

> I can't believe you think perfectly nice people should be put in jail for using social media.

BANDWAGON ARGUMENT //////////

This type of argument makes the claim that something must be true because it's popular or many people believe it.

> Everyone in my class is on social media, and they love it.

SLIPPERY SLOPE /////////////

This type of argument assumes that if one thing is allowed to happen, it will automatically cause a chain reaction.

> No way. If we outlaw social media, then pretty soon real-life conversations will be illegal too.

RED HERRING /////////////

In this logical fallacy, instead of addressing the original argument, a person purposely introduces a new argument or claim as a distraction.

> If you really cared about being healthy, you would exercise.

FALSE DILEMMA /////////////

This type of argument wrongly assumes that there are only two possible conclusions to a particular issue. This is sometimes called "black-or-white" thinking.

> Well, we either outlaw social media and stay healthy, or we don't outlaw it, and we turn into mindless blobs.

APPEAL TO EMOTION ///////////

In this fallacy, instead of making a counterargument, a person makes claims that manipulate the other person's emotions.

> That's mean. Think of how hard it will be for people to connect with relatives and friends who live far away.

QUESTIONABLE CAUSE ///////////

This type of argument wrongly assumes that because two different things happened at the same time, one of the things caused the other.

> They outlawed social media, and bullying increased!

QUIZ: NAME THAT FALLACY!

Logical fallacies don't always sound wrong. That's why critical thinking is so important! Use what you've learned on pages 73–76 to identify the logical fallacies in the statements below. Then check out the answers on page 79.

1. "More than half the people in the U.S. believe in aliens, so they must be real."
   a. Questionable cause
   b. Bandwagon argument
   c. False dilemma

2. "It's ok to cheat on this exam. Think of how upset your parents will be if you get a bad grade!"
   a. Slippery slope
   b. Red herring
   c. Appeal to emotion

3. "Well, you either support our political party, or you don't care about the country."
   a. False dilemma
   b. Bandwagon argument
   c. Questionable cause

4. "If I don't finish this assignment, I won't get into college, and I'll never get a good job."

    a. Appeal to emotion

    b. Slippery slope

    c. Red herring

5. "Yesterday I had a headache, but then I drank some orange juice, and it went away. Orange juice is a great cure for headaches!"

    a. Questionable cause

    b. Red herring

    c. Bandwagon argument

6. "Mayor Shore thinks it's a good idea to raise taxes. She's not very smart."

    a. False dilemma

    b. Ad hominem

    c. Slippery slope

7. "I know you're upset that you didn't get picked for the school musical, but think of all the schools that don't even have a drama club!"

    a. Red herring

    b. Appeal to emotion

    c. Questionable cause

8. "James says that sharks are his favorite animal. I can't believe he doesn't like dolphins!"

    a. Straw-man argument

    b. Ad hominem

    c. Bandwagon argument

ANSWERS

1) b   5) a

2) c   6) b

3) a   7) a

4) b   8) a

"It was a **BIG WAKE-UP CALL** to see **SO MANY** people **AFFECTED BY** [the **AFTER SCHOOL** app] in a **NEGATIVE** way."

—**MOLLY ENGELS,** *STUDENT ACTIVIST AND PRESIDENT OF THE CAMPUS CLUB CYBER YOU*

PORTRAIT OF A CRITICAL THINKER

RUTLAND HIGH STUDENTS

For students at Rutland High School in Vermont, social media opened the door to a big problem: cyberbullying. The popular app After School allowed students to post anonymously about things happening at the school. The creators claimed the app's purpose was to help school communities and students share information about events and local happenings. But at some schools, including Rutland High School, the app became a place where students posted hurtful and negative messages about each other. Many students started to experience intense bullying through the app. Rather than wait for administrators and parents to address the issue, students came together to find a solution. A student-run club called Cyber You promoted responsible digital citizenship. They worked with other students to create a two-part strategy. First they petitioned the app creators to delete their school's message board from the app. Then the students launched a positivity campaign at their school. People were invited to write encouraging and positive messages to each other and post them around the school. The students' activism soon captured national attention. Vermont governor Peter Shumlin said, "The students' campaign makes me realize that people of all ages can do the right thing, and doing so can send a powerful message."

YOUR TURN

Let's practice evaluating evidence. What do you think about social-media use? Is it healthy or unhealthy, neither, or both? Spend 15 minutes doing some research on the topic. Write down all the claims you find on a piece of paper. Then use what you've learned in this chapter to evaluate the claims. Are you any closer to reaching a conclusion?

"You never **REALLY** **UNDERSTAND** a **PERSON** until you **CONSIDER THINGS** from his **POINT OF VIEW**... until you **CLIMB** into **HIS SKIN** and **WALK AROUND** in it."

—**HARPER LEE,** A WRITER WHO WON A PULITZER PRIZE FOR HER NOVEL TO KILL A MOCKINGBIRD, WHICH EXPLORED RACISM DURING THE JIM CROW ERA

Chapter -5-

Getting Curious

You might think that once you find information and evaluate it, it's time to make a decision about a particular issue. Of course, as you collect knowledge, it's totally natural to start drawing some conclusions. But don't sprint to the finish line just yet! There's an important phase *after* you evaluate evidence and *before* you reach a conclusion. You might call it the "getting curious" phase.

During this phase, smart thinkers:

Consider other points of view

Examine their own point of view

Understand the power of emotion

Practice empathy

Immigration

If you live in the United States, chances are there's an immigrant in your family tree. The immigrant might be you or maybe a parent. Or maybe the immigrants in your family are further out—your grandparents or great-grandparents or distant cousins. Our country's past and present are full of immigrant stories.

What is an immigrant exactly? The simple definition is a person who leaves the country where he or she was born and moves to a new country. All countries have immigrants because people—for many different reasons—are always moving from one country to another. *Refugee* is the name for a person who moves to a new country because their own country has become unsafe due to war, violence, or natural disasters. In recent years, stories about immigrants and refugees have been in the national news more and more. Like climate change and other issues we've covered in this book, immigration issues bring up many different opinions and emotions in people. Sometimes it's hard to think clearly when big emotions like fear and anger get involved. (In this chapter, you'll learn what you can do about that.) But thinking something through will help you know what to do with those big emotions.

TIME TO THINK

Here are some questions that might come up when people start talking about immigration.

How do we decide who's allowed to move to our country and who's not?

What does it mean to be undocumented?

How long does it take someone to become a citizen? Is it easy or difficult? Why?

What's deportation?

What are some reasons people have for moving to our country?

What happens if we don't let refugees into our country? What happens if we do?

In what ways do immigrants contribute to our country? In what ways do they harm it?

Do you know the answers to any of these complicated questions? If not, is there a way you can find out?

Considering Other Points of View

As you read in the previous chapter, one reason people reach different conclusions—despite having the same evidence—is that each person has a different point of view or perspective on a particular issue. Let's start with a simple example. Imagine you're at a theater watching a musical. Your experience of the show—and literal point of view—will be different depending on who you are and where you sit. An audience member in the front row will have a different perspective (and experience) from an audience member in the very last row of the balcony.

Now let's revisit this idea using immigration. The decisions a person makes about immigration-related issues will be different depending on who they are and what their perspective is. Consider the question, "How do we decide who's allowed to move to our country and who's not?" How might the following people have different perspectives? Write down your answers on a piece of paper. Do you personally know any of the following people? If so, you might ask them to share their point of view with you.

An immigrant who just arrived in the U.S.

A person whose parents are undocumented immigrants and moved to the U.S. before she was born

A person who lives near the U.S. border

A person who has never met an immigrant

A person who has had only bad interactions with people who are immigrants

A person who has had only good interactions with people who are immigrants

> A refugee who has left her country because of war

Examining Your Own Point of View

In critical thinking, there's another point of view you should consider too—yours! No matter the question or issue, each of us has our own point of view, and it's worth examining what that is and how it came to be. Our point of view is made up of our own knowledge and life experiences. But take a closer look, and you'll find two more things to examine: your assumptions and inferences.

An *assumption* is a belief that a person thinks is true without questioning if it's true.

An *inference* is a conclusion a person makes based on evidence they've gathered or an assumption they have.

For example, you see a friend go to the nurse's office at school, and you conclude that she must be sick. Your assumption is people go to the school nurse when they're sick. Your inference is your friend went to the school nurse, so she must be sick.

A Real-World Example

Our assumptions play a part in shaping our point of view. But they can't always be trusted. Assumptions and inferences can be right, but they can also be wrong or based on false evidence. That's why it's important to get curious about them. In the example below, look at the different ways a person's assumption can influence their reaction to a new immigrant family moving to the neighborhood.

NEIGHBOR #1 / / / / / / / / / / /

Assumption: There's never a good reason for a person to leave their home country.

Inference: The immigrant family who left their home country must have a bad reason for leaving. They're probably running from the police.

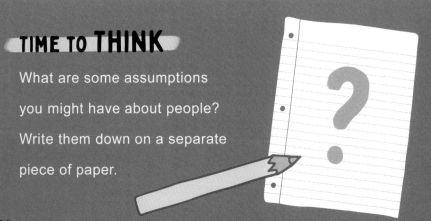

TIME TO THINK

What are some assumptions you might have about people? Write them down on a separate piece of paper.

NEIGHBOR #2 /////////////

Assumption: Most new immigrants can't understand English.

Inference: I'm afraid to introduce myself because they probably won't understand what I'm saying.

NEIGHBOR #3 /////////////

Assumption: It's difficult to be an immigrant in an unfamiliar country.

Inference: The next time I see my new neighbors outside, I'm going to invite them over for dinner.

Understanding the Power of Emotion

Emotions—joy, sadness, anger, hope, and all the rest— are neither good nor bad on their own. Yet they can be very powerful. They can lead people to say and do amazing things and also terrible things (and a lot of other things between the two extremes).

In an argument (remember the definition from page 73?), emotions can be used to inspire people or convince them to change their minds. Emotions can also be used to try to control people and what they think. This is actually another type of logical fallacy called *appeal to emotion*. In this fallacy, a person purposely—and often unfairly—

tries to create an emotional response in someone, instead of creating an argument that can be debated. There's nothing wrong with trying to get someone to see your point of view. But there's a difference between:

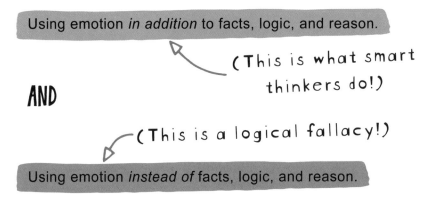

Using emotion *in addition* to facts, logic, and reason.

(This is what smart thinkers do!)

AND

(This is a logical fallacy!)

Using emotion *instead of* facts, logic, and reason.

It's not always easy to spot the appeal-to-emotion fallacy in action, but there are ways to do it. When you hear or read an argument, be on the lookout for this pattern.

A claim ➡ An emotional appeal ➡ A call to action

Notice what's missing? There are no evidence or facts presented.

Here are two opposing arguments about whether or not to let refugees into the United States.

"We're letting too many refugees into this country. I talked to my neighbor last week and he got fired from his job, and now he can't afford to buy groceries or pay his rent. It's awful. We need to stop letting people into this country so we don't all lose our jobs."

"We're not letting enough refugees into this country. I saw a story on social media about a family who had to leave their country because of a war, and now they're homeless. What are they supposed to do? We need to let more refugees into this country so they can be safe."

These are two opposing arguments, yet they are both examples of the appeal-to-emotion fallacy. They include a claim, an emotional appeal, and a call to action. BUT, neither one is a sound argument because both are missing evidence and logic.

Want one more tip for spotting the appeal-to-emotion fallacy? Notice if someone's argument makes you feel afraid or angry. Anytime someone such as a politician or person on the news or social media says something that makes you feel very afraid or very angry, that's a good time to pause and get curious about the emotions they're appealing to.

Is the person making a sound argument? Or are they using a logical fallacy to mess with your emotions?

Empathy

The last step is to practice empathy, and actually, it's something you've been learning about throughout this whole chapter. What is empathy?

THE BiG iDEA

EMPATHY iS THE ABiLiTY TO iMAGiNE AND UNDERSTAND ANOTHER PERSON'S THOUGHTS, FEELiNGS, AND EXPERiENCES. SOME PEOPLE REFER TO iT AS "PUTTiNG YOURSELF iN SOMEONE ELSE'S SHOES."

Practicing empathy while we pursue smart thinking helps us remember that there are people behind the opinions, arguments, and news stories. You practice empathy when you consider someone else's point of view, consider your own point of view, and get curious about emotions. Because most of the time, if you look behind opinions and arguments, you'll see people who want to be heard and understood.

QUIZ: SOUND ARGUMENT OR APPEAL TO EMOTION?

It's not always easy to tell if a person is using emotion within an argument or in place of an argument. Read these statements and see if you can spot the difference between a sound argument and a logical fallacy.

1. "I know I told Mom that I'd pick you up from practice, but I seriously had the worst day. You won't believe what happened to me at lunch!"
   - Sound argument
   - Appeal to emotion

2. "It's not fair that the whole class got punished because a couple people didn't follow the rules. We're upset because most of us turned in the assignment on time."
   - Sound argument
   - Appeal to emotion

3. "If I were elected class president, I would create a campaign to stop bullying. There are some kids who are

afraid to come to school! Our school counselor says that more than half the people in our school have been bullied."
- Sound argument
- Appeal to emotion

4. "The city should do something about the water pollution in Pine Creek. Think of the poor fish that have to live in that dirty water!"
- Sound argument
- Appeal to emotion

5. "You should really wear your seatbelt. Imagine if you were in an accident. Wearing a seatbelt reduces your risk of injury by 45 percent."
- Sound argument
- Appeal to emotion

6. "Sugar isn't good for you. If you eat too much, all your teeth will rot and fall out."
- Sound argument
- Appeal to emotion

7. "If we don't pass this law, something terrible will happen!"
- Sound argument
- Appeal to emotion

"The first time I **SHARED MY STORY** was a **COMPLETE RELEASE,** like coming out of that **SECRECY...** Seeing how the **COMMUNITY SUPPORTED ME,** my **FRIENDS** and my **TEACHERS,** that filled me with **HOPE** that a **CHANGE** can be **GENERATED.**"

—**CRISTINA JIMÉNEZ MORETA,**

A SOCIAL JUSTICE ORGANIZER AND COFOUNDER

OF THE COUNTRY'S LARGEST YOUTH-LED

ORGANIZATION FOR IMMIGRANT RIGHTS

PORTRAIT OF A CRITICAL THINKER

CRISTINA JIMÉNEZ MORETA

When Cristina Jiménez Moreta was a young teen, her parents packed up their family and moved to the United States from Ecuador. Their life in Ecuador had been difficult. Cristina's parents believed they needed to move to the U.S. so that Cristina and her brother could escape poverty and receive a good education. But when Cristina's parents arrived in New York, they were undocumented immigrants—and Cristina and her brother were too. It was a scary time in their lives. They couldn't return to Ecuador, yet there wasn't a clear path to becoming U.S. citizens. Life in the U.S. as an undocumented immigrant was difficult for Cristina. She describes living in fear of police, of having wages stolen by employers, and of deportation. When Cristina grew up and attended college, she began to share her immigration story and learned there were other people with stories like hers. But her work didn't stop with sharing experiences. Cristina began to organize fellow immigrants and develop a way to make their voices heard by people in government. She cofounded United We Dream, an organization that advocates for undocumented immigrants across the United States. In

YOUR TURN

One easy way to exercise your empathy muscle is to read about someone else's life. Just head to the library and check out an autobiography or biography. (An autobiography is the story someone writes about their own life. A biography is a book about someone else's life.) Make a list of people from the past and present that you would like to learn more about. Then ask a librarian to help you find their life stories!

Even when you're young, you still have a story to tell and a point of view to share. Try writing your own autobiography—type it, handwrite it, illustrate it, or turn it into a graphic novel. It might help you to better

2018, Cristina made the *Time* 100 list, *Time* magazine's annual list of the 100 most influential people in the world, for her work on behalf of immigrants.

understand yourself and how you look at the world. Here are some things you might want to include in your story:

Where and when you were born

A description of your family

The funniest thing that ever happened to you

A challenge you had to overcome

A description of your friends

Your dreams for the future

What you like to do for fun

"The **KEY** to good **DECISION MAKING** is not **KNOWLEDGE**. It is **UNDERSTANDING**."

–**MALCOLM GLADWELL,** *A JOURNALIST AND AUTHOR WHO STUDIES HOW PEOPLE THINK AND MAKE DECISIONS*

Chapter
-6-

Drawing Conclusions

We've finally arrived at the step many people try to reach too quickly in the critical thinking process. As we've said before, it can be *really* tempting to take a shortcut from asking questions to drawing conclusions. But think of all the steps—and important info—you would miss in between! Let's review where we've been.

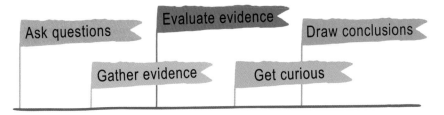

Critical Thinking Process

Now it's time to draw a conclusion. (You can also think of this as making a decision or figuring out an answer.)

THE BiG iDEA

DRAWING A CONCLUSION IS THE LAST STEP IN THE CRITICAL THINKING PROCESS. IT'S BASED ON REASON AND EVIDENCE.

The Self-Care Trend

Wellness is a popular topic these days. You've probably heard plenty of adults talking about the healthy things you should do for your body and mind, like eating nutritious food, staying active, and meditating. You've also probably heard people talking about harmful things to avoid, such as alcohol and drugs. Sometimes the topic of wellness sounds like just more rules we need to follow, but there are really good reasons to think about these things. How we treat our bodies and minds—and what we put into them—affects many parts of our lives. It can affect how we feel, what we think, the choices we make, and our relationships with others.

No matter who we are, each of us has physical and mental needs (though they're so closely related to each other, they're basically the same thing). People often disagree on how to meet those needs, or even whether or not they're important. When it comes to wellness, you'll probably hear a lot of conflicting opinions and ideas. That's why critical thinking is so important.

Healthy Habits

What are some ways you care for your body and mind? Choose some of your favorites from the list below and write them in a notebook. Refer back to them when you're having a bad day or not quite feeling like yourself. (Because that happens to everyone!)

Eat healthy food.

Drink plenty of water.

Get some exercise.

Get good sleep.

Share your feelings and thoughts with others.

Spend time with animals.

Spend time in nature.

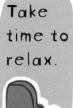

Take time to relax.

Set limits for screen time.

Practice mindfulness.

Express yourself with art, writing, music, or dance.

Do something just for fun.

TIME TO **THINK**

Mindfulness simply means focusing on the present moment, especially what you notice with your five senses. Here's a quick way to do it. Sit down on a chair or on the floor. Close your eyes. Take a deep breath. Hold it for two seconds, then slowly breathe out. Repeat this about five times. You can use this exercise whenever your brain needs a break!

How to Draw a Conclusion

As you draw a conclusion, it's important to:

Revisit your original question

Review the evidence and what you've learned

Consider your values

Another step you might want to add?

Take a breather!

Thinking for yourself is hard work. Sometimes it can be good to just take a brain break. (Try one of the activities on pages 107–108 if you need ideas!)

Consider Your Values

A value is a personal belief that you think is important. Individuals, families, and other groups of people can all have their own values. Our values almost always play a part in our decisions. In fact, values can actually help us make decisions. On the next page are some examples of values that people may have.

HONESTY ////////////

> I think people should always tell the truth about what they're thinking and feeling.

KINDNESS ////////////

> I'm not going to cancel my plans with Lucy to hang out with Isabel and Max.

TIMELINESS ////////////

> We're going to leave five minutes early so that Grandma doesn't have to wait for us.

HEALTH ////////////

> I go to bed early because I want to make sure I get enough sleep.

What do you think your family's values might be? Or your own? Do any of these values contradict each other or lead to different conclusions? Not sure? Try the activity on page 114.

Putting It into Practice

Imagine you overhear some classmates talking about smoking and vaping. They're arguing about whether or not these habits are actually bad for people. One classmate says that vaping (using e-cigarettes) is less dangerous than smoking because there's no smoke. A second classmate disagrees. Then your teacher overhears and says vaping is unhealthy and dangerous. You? You've never really thought about it until now. But as you sit there listening, you wonder,

> Why is vaping bad for you?
> I mean, it is bad for you, right?

And just like that, you've started thinking for yourself!

Let's say after you asked the question, you decided to investigate, and now it's time to draw a conclusion. Critical thinking often happens all in your head.

(Sometimes if a question is extra challenging, it helps to write things down.) When you review your critical

REVISIT THE ORIGINAL QUESTION.

"Is vaping bad for you?"

REVIEW THE EVIDENCE AND WHAT YOU LEARNED FROM IT.

Talked to Ethan. He says it's not bad for you, but it turns out his only source was his older brother Shawn. Hmm.

Asked Ms. Watkins why she said vaping is bad. She said that e-cigarettes contain nicotine, which is very addictive. She showed me where I can read some articles about it.

thinking process—in your head or on paper—it might look something like this.

Read the articles that Ms. Watkins showed me. Two of them were written by doctors. Watched a couple videos online about it.

CONSIDER YOUR VALUES.

Being Healthy: I play volleyball, so it's important that I feel my best.

Respecting the Law: Smoking and vaping are both illegal for people who are under the age of 18 (and in some states, the age is even higher).

Independence: I like thinking for myself. I'm not going to do something just because my classmates are doing it.

QUIZ: ARE YOU READY TO MAKE A DECISION?

Yes.

Find this on page 73.

A what?

Did you evaluate and investigate your evidence?

Do you know what a logical fallacy is?

Done!

Yep.

Of course!

Did you take time to get curious, practice empathy, and consider other points of view?

Uh...

You're ready to decide!

Visit page 96!

Check!

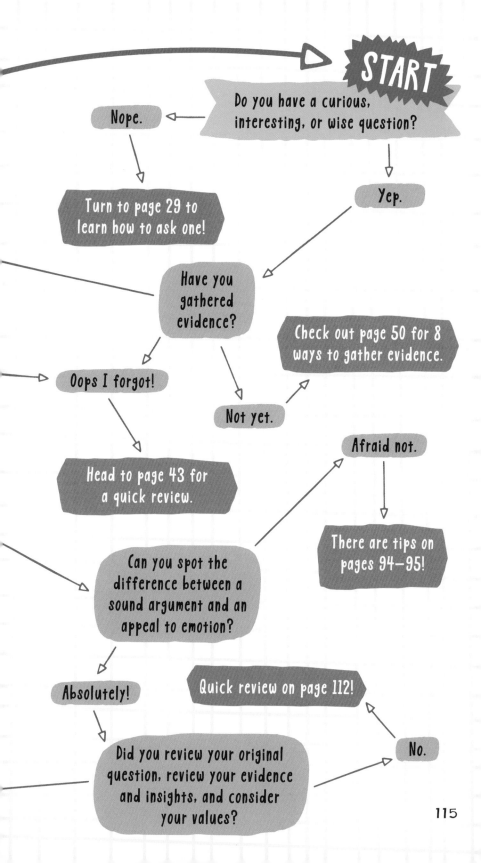

START

Do you have a curious, interesting, or wise question?

Nope.

Turn to page 29 to learn how to ask one!

Yep.

Have you gathered evidence?

Check out page 50 for 8 ways to gather evidence.

Oops I forgot!

Not yet.

Afraid not.

Head to page 43 for a quick review.

There are tips on pages 94–95!

Can you spot the difference between a sound argument and an appeal to emotion?

Absolutely!

Quick review on page 112!

Did you review your original question, review your evidence and insights, and consider your values?

No.

"**MENTAL HEALTH PROBLEMS DON'T DEFINE** who **YOU** are... They are **SOMETHING** you **EXPERIENCE**... You **WALK** in the **RAIN** and you **FEEL** the **RAIN,** but

–IMPORTANT–
YOU ARE NOT the **RAIN.**"

–**MATT HAIG,** A MENTAL HEALTH ADVOCATE
AND AUTHOR WHO WRITES BOOKS FOR
CHILDREN AND ADULTS

PORTRAIT OF A CRITICAL THINKER

MATT HAIG

When writer Matt Haig was growing up in England in the 1980s, people didn't talk about mental health. Things like depression or anxiety were secrets people were expected to keep to themselves. At the time, there wasn't a lot of information about what caused these mental health issues or what could be done to help people. When Matt was in school, he felt anxious and had a hard time fitting in and making friends. As a teen, he started using drugs and alcohol as a way to deal with his feelings and fit in with others. But when Matt was a young man, he experienced depression and anxiety in scary ways. At first, Matt didn't know what to do. He was afraid to talk about it. Slowly, however, he began to tell people in his life about his struggles. He stopped using drugs and alcohol. He started learning about the connection between how he treated his mind and body and how he felt. He began to understand his unique personality and how to best care for it. Eventually, he felt much better. Now, many years later, Matt writes books for children and adults. (Some of his books are even being turned into movies.) But one of Matt's biggest accomplishments has been challenging stereotypes about mental health. His critical thinking has helped change our conversation about mental health and given other people hope when they're facing hard times.

YOUR TURN

What are your values? If you're not sure, it might help to ask your parents about their values or what they hope your family values as a group. You could also ask a teacher, friend, or someone else in your life. Here is a list of some common values that people have. In a notebook, write down the ones that are important to you. Then come up with some more on your own! Keep it somewhere close and read it later when you're struggling to make a decision.

Peace

Honesty

Courage

Open-mindedness

Community

Loyalty

Hard work

Respect

Determination

Creativity

119

"You can **DISAGREE** without **BEING** **DISAGREEABLE.**"

—**RUTH BADER GINSBURG,** A U.S.

SUPREME COURT JUSTICE WHO ADVOCATES

FOR GENDER EQUALITY

DISCUSSING

Other Points of View

Drawing a conclusion might be the end of the critical thinking process, but it isn't the end of all thinking. Our decisions, beliefs, and thoughts don't exist on an island all by themselves. They're part of the real world, and there are usually consequences for our decisions and beliefs. No matter how sure we are of our own conclusions, we will meet people who come to different conclusions. We will meet people who disagree with us. Then what? That's what this chapter is all about.

School Safety

How can we make our schools safe for students and teachers? It's a question that comes up a lot in public debate. In fact, it's a question that's been continually asked in the United States for at least a few decades. Today there are many activists dedicated to making schools safer. Most people agree that the problem of gun violence in schools is so serious that the United States government needs to be involved in solving the problem. But what does that mean? What kind of laws can be passed to stop the violence? Should laws be passed? Why has it taken so long to solve our country's problem with gun violence? What do other countries do? As you can see, this is a topic that brings up a lot of questions. It also brings up a lot of opinions. And these opinions can lead to intense discussions and debate—both online and in our communities.

Keep It to Yourself or Go Public?

When you reach a conclusion about something (even a big issue like school safety or climate change), it's ok to keep that information to yourself. Whether you share it or not, it's most important to simply know your own mind and what you think. (You still get credit for being a smart thinker!) When the time comes to share your point of view, here are some ways you can do that.

Discuss it with someone.

Debate with someone.
(More on this on page 132!)

Write an email or letter.

Make art.

Write a story or article.

Of course, sometimes it's true that actions speak louder than words. Showing your point of view with the choices you make and the way you live your life is one of the most powerful things you can do.

How to Share Your Point of View

When it's time for you to speak up, there's an important word you might want to keep in mind. It's an old-fashioned word. In fact, historians can trace it back hundreds of years.

The word is *civility*.

In English, we think of civility as being polite or having good manners. But the word's original meaning (in Latin!) is more interesting and complicated than that. Originally, practicing civility meant to act in a way that contributes to the common good. It had to do with being a good citizen in a community and helping that community thrive.

It's an idea that's still worth considering today. Especially when we start talking about difficult or sensitive topics.

Being civil doesn't mean you hide your opinions or put on a mask of good manners. It means sharing your opinions and ideas in a way that contributes to the common good. It's actually more about the way you share your ideas and treat other people than about the ideas themselves.

THE BiG iDEA

PEOPLE CAN DISAGREE AND STILL BE RESPECTFUL AND KIND TO EACH OTHER.

When you share your point of view with someone, it's important to also listen to their point of view. Listening is a skill you probably started learning a looooong time ago. So you might think you should be pretty good at it by now. But listening is a life skill, so it's not something you learn once and then it's over. Listening is a skill you practice throughout your life, even as an adult. Active listeners are:

Engaged
They use facial expressions and body language, such as nodding or leaning forward, to show they're paying attention.

Curious
They know when to stay quiet, but they also ask thought-provoking questions such as "Why do you feel that way?" and use phrases like "Tell me more about that." They often ask "What can I learn here?"

Kind
They show they care about the person who's talking, even when they disagree with what's being said. (Body language, facial expressions, and tone of voice go a long way in showing kindness to someone.)

Focused
They put away distractions like phones when they're in a conversation.

TIME TO THINK

Which of the following scenes shows an active listener?

How to Debate

What happens if you share your conclusion about something and someone tells you that you're wrong? What if someone comes to a conclusion that you think is wrong? This is tricky, no matter who you are. In certain situations, it's best to just let things go. People can spend a lot of time debating and arguing online with strangers they'll never know or see. Most of the time, social media isn't a good place to have important debates. (And P.S.: Sometimes the "people" that say shocking things or start arguments online aren't even real people. They're just bots designed to stir up trouble and make people angry. And they're *really* good at it.)

If you're in a face-to-face situation where you want to debate another person's argument, here's how to go about it.

Know Your Audience

Understand that people might be sensitive about certain topics depending on their life experiences. Ask the person you disagree with if he or she is open to a conversation.

Consider the Setting

Are you in a place where it's comfortable to have a discussion? Places that are too loud or too busy can be distracting when you're trying to talk about something that's important.

Know Your Facts

If the other person brings up something you don't have the answer to, tell them you'll look into it and get back to them later.

Ask Questions

Try to clarify the areas you agree and disagree about. You'll help both sides understand the ideas more deeply.

Stay on Topic

If you veer off course, make sure to come back to your original argument.

Play Fair

Avoid name-calling and personal insults. Focus on learning and connecting rather than winning.

Be a Good Listener

Give other people the chance to respond and share their point of view.

QUIZ: SHOULD YOU SPEAK UP?

In the moment, it can be hard to know if you should speak up or let things go. This checklist will help you practice. If you can answer yes to all these questions, you're good to go. If not, think about how you might say something later or in a different way so your ideas can truly be heard.

☐ You feel calm, and the situation is safe.

☐ You know the other people in the discussion well.

☐ You're having a discussion in real life.

☐ You have done some research and know the facts or have personal experience with the topic.

☐ Everyone has time to talk through the issue.

☐ People are interested and ready to talk about the topic.

☐ You're more interested in learning and connecting than winning.

"I most definitely **FEEL HOPEFUL** because I've met so many **PEOPLE** who are **READY** to **ENGAGE** in our **POLITICAL SYSTEM,** and these are **EXACTLY** the **PEOPLE WE NEED** to engage. **PEOPLE** who are **DEVOTED** to the concept of **KEEPING** people **SAFE**...People who are **LOOKING OUT** for **EACH OTHER, NOT** just **THEMSELVES."**

—EMMA GONZÁLEZ, *A STUDENT ACTIVIST WHO HELPED START A POLITICAL MOVEMENT AFTER A DEADLY SHOOTING AT HER SCHOOL*

PORTRAIT OF A CRITICAL THINKER
EMMA GONZÁLEZ

As a high school senior, Emma González was looking ahead to college and thinking about her future. She was an ordinary teenager—until a tragic shooting at her school changed her life. The shooting was national news, but for Emma and her friends, it was very personal. They lost 17 classmates and teachers. Emma was deeply sad and angry. Yet a few days later at a rally, she found the courage to give a speech, calling on politicians to pass tighter gun-control laws. Her emotional words made headlines. Emma was surprised and directed the attention to her campaign for tighter gun-control laws. She went on to help organize March for Our Lives, the national student-led demonstration. Now in college, she uses her voice to speak out against gun violence and inspires others to do the same.

YOUR TURN

A formal debate is different than the kind of informal debate we discussed on page 126. You may have seen formal debates on TV between political candidates, or your school may have a debate team. Debating is a good skill to practice. If you want, you can host a debate yourself or ask your teacher if you can have one in your classroom. Here are the basic ground rules.

Before the Debate

1. Choose a topic to debate. This could be a national issue such as immigration laws or a more local issue such as, "Should our school allow students to eat lunch off campus?"

2. Divide into two groups. If you're doing this in a classroom, ask half your classmates to be on the affirmative side and half to be on the negative side. (In this example, this means that half the class should prepare to debate in favor of open lunch and half should prepare to debate against open lunch.)

3. Give each side time to research their arguments. It helps to do this a couple days before the formal debate.

During the Debate

Follow this basic schedule. (It's ok to vary it too. Debates can follow a variety of formats.)

1. The affirmative side gets 2 minutes to present their argument.

2. The negative side gets 2 minutes to present their argument.

3. The affirmative side gets 2 minutes to present their rebuttal and summary.

4. The negative side gets 2 minutes to present their rebuttal and summary.

5. The audience (or teacher) decides who presented the stronger argument. Whoever presented the stronger argument wins the debate.

*In formal debates (such as school debate teams), students don't always get to debate from the point of view they agree with. It's actually good practice to learn how to debate different sides of the same issue.

"One's **MIND,** once **STRETCHED** by a **NEW IDEA, NEVER REGAINS** its **ORIGINAL DIMENSIONS.**"

—**OLIVER WENDELL HOLMES,** *A POET AND PHYSICIAN WHO WAS KNOWN FOR HIS WRITING AND INFLUENCE ON MEDICINE*

Growing

Critical thinking isn't only about finding answers or drawing conclusions; it's about learning and growing. This may be the end of the book, but that doesn't mean it should go back on a shelf. (Unless you're borrowing it from the library!) This is a guide you can read again and again as you practice thinking for yourself in the real world.

In the previous chapter we talked about what to do when someone tells you that you're wrong or you disagree with someone else's opinion. It's ok to discuss or debate ideas with people, as long as you remember to do things such as ask good questions, stay on topic, and be kind. But there's another thing it's ok to do too: change your mind. It's common—and healthy—to come to a conclusion, then discover new information or meet a person who changes your mind about that conclusion. This is how we learn and grow.

Great thinkers are always growing.

Pitfalls

Even when you think you've mastered the critical thinking process, you can still make mistakes. Here's what to do when you run into one of these common pitfalls.

YOUR CONCLUSION IS WRONG

See it as an opportunity to learn. It doesn't hurt to go back and review how you ended up at the conclusion. (And keep in mind that not all issues have a clear right or wrong answer.)

YOU HURT SOMEONE'S FEELINGS

Just because your conversation or debate makes someone upset doesn't mean it's your fault. Yet at some point, we all say hurtful things because we don't know better. If you're in a conversation with someone and they're upset, try to understand why. And if it's because of something you did or said, it's a good idea to apologize.

YOUR FEELINGS GET HURT

Consider telling the person or taking a break from the conversation to clear your head. Using the phrase "That hurts my feelings" can remind others we are all human.

IT GETS AWKWARD

Pause to see if any awkward silences might give people time to think. Or laugh it off. A joke or humor can go a long way! If that doesn't feel right, check in to make sure the person is ok, or simply change the subject. Sometimes it's better to move on and talk about something else.

We all think in different ways. Some people need a lot of time to think, others don't. Some people need quiet, others need music or background noise. How about you? Read this checklist to help you figure out how you do your best thinking.

I DO MY BEST THINKING WHEN...

- ☐ It's quiet.
- ☐ There's background noise.
- ☐ I can write or type my thoughts.
- ☐ I'm drawing or doodling.
- ☐ I'm listening to music.
- ☐ I'm alone.
- ☐ I'm with other people.
- ☐ I'm inside.
- ☐ I'm outside.
- ☐ I'm moving.
- ☐ I'm still.
- ☐ I have a lot of time.

TIME TO THINK

You probably had a lot on your mind before you started reading this book. And now? You might have even more! Sometimes it helps to write down our thoughts, even when we don't fully understand them yet. Use a notebook and the following prompts to help you. (Do one, all, or none—whatever is helpful to you!)

What do you think about when your mind wanders?

Who do you know that's good at answering questions?

Who do you know that's good at asking questions?

What big issues do you think about the most?

What small issues do you think about the most?

Who's a thinker that you admire? What makes them so smart?

Is there a part of critical thinking you don't understand?

Did this book help you come to any conclusions or make any decisions? What are they?

What will you remember most from this book?

THE BiG iDEA

CRITICAL THINKING IS THE PROCESS OF CAREFULLY EVALUATING IDEAS AND FACTS TO MAKE DECISIONS ABOUT WHAT TO BELIEVE AND DO.

ASK QUESTIONS

It's normal to wonder about the world around us. All critical thinking starts with at least one question.

GATHER EVIDENCE

Evidence is the information that helps you find an answer or make a decision. There are many ways to collect it.

EVALUATE EVIDENCE

Smart thinkers evaluate the importance, accuracy, and relevancy of the information they gather. Watch out for logical fallacies!

GET CURIOUS

Consider different conclusions and other points of view.

DRAW CONCLUSIONS

Drawing a conclusion is the last step in the critical thinking process. It's based on reason and evidence.

DISCUSS AND DEBATE

No matter how sure we are of our own conclusions, we will meet people who come to different conclusions. People can disagree and still be respectful and kind to each other.

KEEP GROWING

Thinking critically isn't only about finding answers or drawing conclusions; it's about learning and growing.

This book is all about the tools you need to think for yourself.

Logical Fallacy Detector

Empathy

Research

Listening

Time to Think

A New Point of View

Stereotype Buster

Assumption Tester

So now what do you do with these tools?

YOU decide!

Glossary

activist A person who uses strong action in favor of or against a particular cause.

argument In critical thinking, a series of statements that are meant to support a particular conclusion.

assumption A belief that a person thinks is true without questioning if it's true.

autobiography The story of someone's life written by himself or herself.

biography The story of someone's life.

civility To be polite or to act in a way that contributes to the common good.

conclusion The end result or outcome; a judgment.

critical thinking The process of carefully evaluating ideas and facts to make decisions about what to believe and do.

debate A discussion of opposing viewpoints.

diversity Variety; the inclusion of many different types of people.

empathy The ability to imagine and understand another person's thoughts, feelings, and experiences.

evidence Information that helps you find an answer or make a decision.

fact A statement that can be verified.

fact-check To research information to find out if it can be verified and if its sources are reliable.

fake news False news stories that are created to purposely mislead and misinform.

immigrant A person who leaves the country where he or she was born and moves to a new country.

inference A conclusion based on evidence and/or assumptions.

logic A way of combining information in order to reach a conclusion.

logical fallacy An error in thinking that weakens or discredits an argument.

mindfulness The practice of focusing on the present moment and what you can notice with your five senses.

opinion A statement of belief.

point of view A position or perspective.

qualitative evidence Information that describes something.

quantitative evidence Information that comes from numbers or statistics; also called data.

reason In philosophy, to use evidence and experiments to find truths or theories.

refugee A person who moves to a new country because their own country has become unsafe due to war, violence, or natural disasters.

social justice The idea and practice of advocating for equality among people in a society.

sources Anything or anyone that provides information; a primary source provides firsthand information while a secondary source provides secondhand information.

stereotype An oversimplified (and often mistaken) belief about a whole group of people based on how they look or limited experience with them.

value A personal belief or quality that you think is important.

wellness The state of being in good health.

Index